Workbook 4 the SOUL

Workbook 4 the SOUL

Deborah M. Robinson

iUniverse, Inc.

New York   Bloomington   Shanghai

Workbook 4 the SOUL

iUniverse books may be ordered through booksellers or by contacting:

iUniverse
1663 Liberty Drive
Bloomington, IN 47403
www.iuniverse.com
1-800-Authors (1-800-288-4677)

Because of the dynamic nature of the Internet, any Web addresses or links contained in this book may have changed since publication and may no longer be valid.

The views expressed in this work are solely those of the author and do not necessarily reflect the views of the publisher, and the publisher hereby disclaims any responsibility for them.

ISBN: 978-0-595-45554-6 (pbk)
ISBN: 978-0-595-89860-2 (ebk)

Printed in the United States of America

Introduction

Workbook 4 the Soul© is meant to feed your spirit, evoke your mind, and inspire your heart. I hope you see the value and understand the purpose.

Early in my life, I was focused on being a good athlete and I played several sports. Even though I hated running track, I did it to learn discipline and to stay in shape. I learned early to make a commitment and to stick with it. Although some people said I could do nothing but sports, I decided to commit to every dream that spoke to my heart. Perseverance has taken me many places. This is one of the many reasons I wrote this book. It was one of those dreams that spoke to my heart.

The message of this book touched my soul and would not release me. This project has been a long time coming. But it has finally come full circle. As I traveled over the highways, most of this material entered my heart. I would lay it aside, only to have it return again. Therefore I became obedient. I put pen to paper and got wonderful results.

It does not matter what you are faced with on a daily basis, your approach to it can make the difference of whether you succeed or fail. Sometimes we just need to step back and evaluate the situation, *then* make the decision to act.

Sometimes our mothers' untold stories are told
by the way that they look at their children.

Sometimes we may get a glimpse of it
when they rub our heads or stroke our faces.

Sometimes those untold stories are burning within us.
Perhaps this is the catalyst for more stories to be told.

Thanks to all who have touched my spirit. The list isn't long, but it's profound. So again, thanks.

To *Marnée*—a powerful woman who has touched my life and allowed me to continue spreading my wings.

My dearest *Michael*—I do love you—continue to learn as you grow, seek knowledge and understanding for I shall always be your greatest supporter.

To my *mother*—who has continued to give me everlasting love and comfort. I adore you more and more each day. I only hope my light shines as bright as yours. Thank you for your patience and for your undivided understanding.

To my siblings, *Ann* and *Frances*—Thanks for being in my world. I'd like to think you are two of the greatest moms I know. And thanks for sharing the ride.

To my inner circle—my dear *friends*—you know me and still love—and that is all that matters.

To *White* and *Eelman*—It is an honor to have been among you. I am in awe of your professionalism.

To my *officiating family*—I am proud to have been among you. It was a great ride ... a world only *stripes* can understand—thanks for the memories.

Many thanks to my *DOP* and *RCC colleagues* who helped me to be the best educator possible. I have enjoyed working along side each of you.

To *Rochelle*—you continue to impress me and I shall forever love you. A heartfelt thanks to *my entire family* whose unwavering love, support, and guidance have allowed me to be myself.

To my three angels—*Darlene*, *Roetta*, and *Barbara*—they taught me the about growth and the gift of healing. To them, I say, "I miss and love you much."

To *Miss Marge*—thanks for your strong support and may God continue to bless you. And to the *children*—you bring us good sunshine and much joy

Most of my life I've been fortunate enough to have formed common bonds with so many people. Without you, I could not have made this journey. I've been told, "**Everyone has a benefactor.**" So, to all of you who have helped open a door for me—I want you to know I am eternally grateful.

Thank you to all of those whose unconditional love allowed me to take the road less traveled and share my findings with them.

And to those of you who have purchased this book,
I hope it does what my soul desired it to do—
I hope it blesses you abundantly.

TRUST

If you've never looked into my eyes, how do you know what's in my heart?

If you know your shepherd,
then why do you still want?
Try believing—it works!

Hollow apologies + empty promises = a lost soul.
Can you find your way back?

Receiving hollow apologies and empty promises on a continual basis can lead to missed opportunities. Don't let life pass you. Decide today that you will trust again.

A critical attitude can cause a divided house.

If God continues to tell us not to doubt,
then why do we continue to
be people of little faith?

Can a race make up a religion?

Why is it so easy for us to strip
one another of our self esteem
when it takes a lifetime to build?

When it comes to domestic violence, are men so macho that we forget they too can be victims?

No one tells them
HOW to leave;
they just tell them to leave.
Let's give them an exit plan.

Do submission and peace have
anything in common?
Think about it!

Is it because men are supposed to be the head that we forget they too are victimized. Drop the image and show him the way.

When passion isn't enough,
you must have a backup plan.
What's yours?

_____

_____
_____
_____
_____
_____
_____
_____
_____
_____
_____
_____
_____
_____
_____
_____
_____
_____
_____
_____
_____
_____
_____
_____
_____
_____
_____
_____
_____

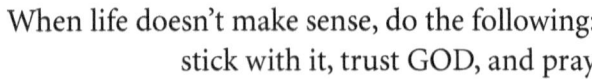

When life doesn't make sense, do the following:
stick with it, trust GOD, and pray

Rhythm breeds LIFE:

Feel (embrace) the beat.

_____

_____

_____

_____

_____

_____

_____

_____

_____

_____

_____

_____

_____

_____

_____

_____

_____

_____

_____

_____

_____

_____

_____

_____

_____

_____

_____

_____

_____

_____

Giving is a precious gift and it's free.
What have you given today?

_____
_____
_____
_____
_____
_____
_____
_____
_____
_____
_____

Name five people you have invested in, and what was the intended lesson?

_____
_____
_____
_____
_____
_____
_____
_____
_____
_____
_____
_____
_____
_____

The difference between a young adult and a teenager is that one has put away childish things and is now looking to become an effective person while the other is still trying to find it or figure it out.

Which one are you?

_____
_____
_____
_____
_____
_____
_____
_____
_____
_____
_____

                    _____
                    _____
                    _____
                    _____

_____
_____
_____
_____
_____
_____
_____
_____
_____
_____
_____
_____
_____

People don't like to take a stand.
They sit the fence or wait
on the crowd to talk about
what needs to be done.
Where do you fit into the equation?

Children want and need to be heard.
But the most important gift to
give them is structure.

Good crews blend in together. Are you blending?

_____

_____

_____

_____

_____

_____

_____

_____

_____

_____

_____

A good leader—
leads
teaches
inspires
seeks opinions
exalts his/her team
never forgets the path that got him/her there

_____

_____

_____

_____

_____

_____

_____

_____

_____

_____

_____

Healing relationships

The key is forgiveness

When relationships are broken, there is much work to be done. We

must first realize that there is a problem. However, we can become so

complacent that we settle for things that are beneath our standards.

Broken relationships occur on several levels, not just marital.

The average person engages in at least four types of relationships
simultaneously.

Heaven forbid they all could be broken or on the brink of breaking.

So what does this do to one's emotions?

How does one maintain

focus and remain productive?

It is virtually impossible, without help.

Let's examine the four relationships: many of us are engaged in

a personal relationship, such as marriage or with a significant other.

Secondly, we're involved in friendships with those that are our best
friends.

Then we speak of kinships—these are relationships that deal

with our children and our siblings. Finally, we have what is known as

our extended relationships; which consist of our co-workers and our church family.

These are people that we spend a significant amount of time with outside of the home.

When these relationships are strained and we become emotionally torn,

we sometimes fall into a rut because we don't know where to turn.

Therefore, we make matters worse by not doing anything or enlisting the wrong help.

When in fact all we have to do is stop and think.

Many times, we don't even know the true condition of the relationship.

However, we should follow three simple steps

when we find ourselves in a broken relationship;

whether it's at home, work, or at church.

Healing needs to take place. If we acknowledge that we have been hurt

and understand the issues that have caused that emotional wound,

then the process has begun.

Secondly, you need to release them from the obligation

and view the truth of the offense.

Thirdly, we must confess why we are bitter and full of resentment.

As we engage in the healing process,

our hearts and minds must be open.

We must be receptive to confronting our fears

and taking a hard look at ourselves.

We must remember for every finger being pointed

there is always one coming back at YOU.

We all have faults, but the beauty of it is

when you can turn things around by accepting

responsibility for your part and relinquish the anger and heal.

That's when we become whole and our relationships are restored unto us.

COMMITMENT

Giving is a precious gift and it's free.
What have you given today?

The past is too expensive to buy back, no one is that rich

You can't love me if you haven't taken care of you.
What do you have to offer me?

_____
_____
_____
_____
_____
_____
_____
_____
_____
_____
_____
_____
_____
_____
_____
_____
_____
_____
_____
_____
_____
_____
_____
_____
_____
_____
_____

Do you know your eyes are
the entrance to your heart?!

Forgiveness is only hard
if you forget to take the step.
Take the step don't let the sun go down
without taking the step!

Blood, sweat, and tears were the price for *freedom* that so many think is *free*.

If you want commitment, invest in a girl!

When you give the world your **best**,
sometimes it will let you down.
Some people accept that while
others find another way.

It's a choice.

_____

_____

_____

_____

_____

_____

_____

_____

_____

_____

_____

_____

_____

_____

_____

_____

_____

_____

_____

_____

_____

_____

_____

_____

_____

Audit your life,
you just might save *it*!

Having never been experienced before,
each second is new so take care of it.

Give it a great memory!

If **you** can't give **100%** then don't go!

Should we encourage children or *empower* them?
Do you know?

How does one know when to change their batteries,
if they don't even know they have any to change?

_____
_____
_____
_____
_____
_____
_____
_____
_____
_____
_____

_____
_____
_____
_____
_____
_____
_____
_____
_____
_____
_____
_____

_____
_____
_____
_____
_____
_____
_____
_____
_____
_____
_____

From the depths of your soul,
lose or win....
by the same power.

_____
_____
_____
_____
_____
_____
_____
_____
_____
_____
_____
_____
_____
_____

Name five strong women you personally know.
How have they inspired you?

1. _____
   _____
   _____
   _____

2. _____
   _____
   _____
   _____

3. _____
   _____
   _____
   _____

4. _____
   _____
   _____
   _____

5. _____
   _____
   _____
   _____

Find a cause.... fill a need!

Take care of business—do not let
death catch you waiting to do it
tomorrow.
Today I am going to....

_____
_____
_____
_____
_____
_____
_____
_____
_____
_____
_____
_____
_____
_____
_____
_____
_____
_____
_____
_____
_____
_____
_____
_____
_____
_____
_____
_____
_____

Dictated by leadership—
dedication, **determination**, and **drive**.
If one component is missing,
the ability to lead will not occur.

Leadership is like effective communication,
    without it we're just like the fan in the window on a hot day
        —just blowing hot air

When *leadership* fails you,
change must arrive

_____

If you call yourself a teacher, you must know what your **message** is!

What are **YOU** doing to save education?

People, places, and things
understand, communicate, and
be flexible!

It is your *duty* to teach someone
because someone stayed the course with you.

_____
_____
_____
_____
_____
_____
_____
_____
_____
_____
_____
_____
_____
_____
_____
_____
_____
_____
_____
_____
_____
_____
_____
_____
_____
_____
_____
_____
_____
_____
_____

Never *indulge* in self without
investing in others.

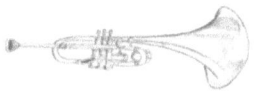

Check that attitude:
you must be honest with self and be able to
question if what you're engaging in is right.
Really stop and think about who you are and
what you are standing for at the present time.

When women don't invest in each other,
we fail ourselves.

Save a nation ~ invest in a girl!

What is *chance* without *change*?

Take a chance on something!

Why would you hold onto
anything that you couldn't let go
of in a hurry?
Today I am releasing:

_____

_____

_____

_____

_____

_____

_____

_____

_____

_____

_____

_____

_____

_____

_____

_____

_____

_____

_____

_____

_____

_____

_____

_____

_____

_____

_____

_____

Students!
Teachers were students at one time
so they really do get it!! Talk to them.

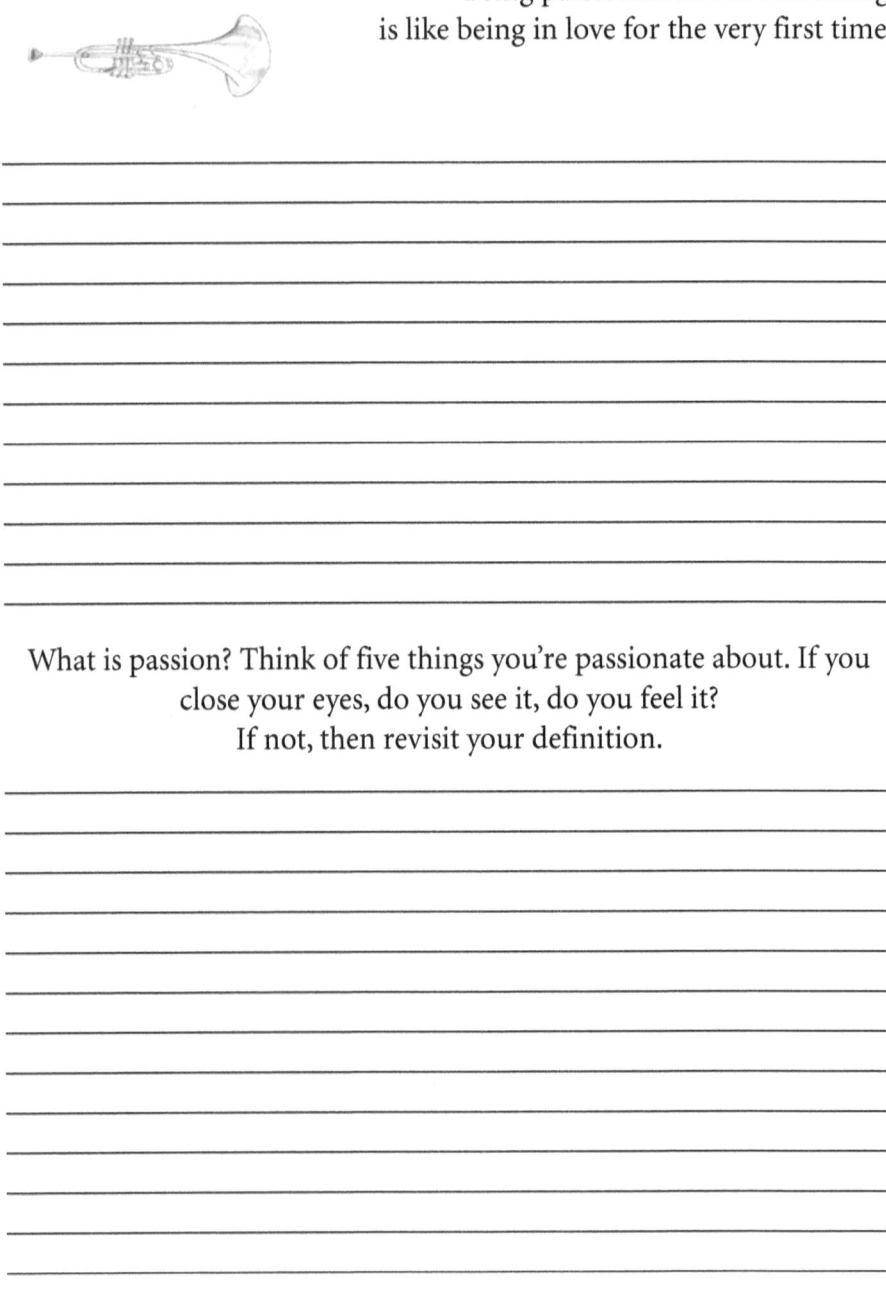

Being passionate about something
is like being in love for the very first time.

_____

_____

_____

_____

_____

_____

_____

_____

_____

_____

What is passion? Think of five things you're passionate about. If you
close your eyes, do you see it, do you feel it?
If not, then revisit your definition.

_____

_____

_____

_____

_____

_____

_____

_____

_____

_____

_____

_____

It should be a top priority to seek understanding,

then be understood.

_____

_____

_____

_____

_____

_____

_____

_____

_____

_____

_____

_____

_____

_____

_____

_____

_____

_____

_____

_____

_____

_____

_____

_____

_____

_____

_____

_____

_____

_____

_____

_____

_____

We are what we continually do,
so if you continually strive for success,
you will know what it feels like.
Today I have taken the following steps …

Visit a museum and see the price of freedom—
it's a daily battle!

Have expectations and anticipate results ... especially from your A_C_T_I_O_N_S.

The world is real. It does not have time to wait for you to find yourself.
Once you enter it, fairness has departed.
In life, there is no fairness.
So get over things not being fair.

When you hear these words,
what kinds of thoughts enter your mind?
Honesty, commitment, loyalty,
potential, quality, and *growth*.

Once you spotted the problem,
what did you do to resolve it?
Talk about it.

What solutions have you
offered for your
complaints today?

Find a way to deal with difficult people …
on your own terms.

Belief—is the interpretation of our experiences that comes from our belief system, and sometimes we **never** question that system because we believe in our hearts it is right. Has you system been evaluated?

Weapons of oppression:
Ignorance, greed, and selfishness.

Please help someone lay these weapons down

Camp is a wonderful thing.
So, children go to camp and
do this while you are there.
Learn, laugh, enjoy yourself,
and make new friends.

SPIRITUAL

Let labels fall: I do not want to be
called a Christian, Jew, or a
Muslim. I just want to follow
God's instructions and do HIS will

Before you begin anything new,
you must first put closure to the past.
You can make the moment you're in rich,
but you must put the past in its proper place.

If the end is coming,
at least know what happened
to the beginning.

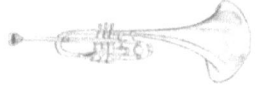

A wondering spirit is one that
can't keep still, always looking
for the other side.
Do you relate?

When you define *dignity*, what do you feel?

_____
_____
_____
_____
_____
_____
_____
_____
_____
_____
_____
_____
_____
_____
_____
_____
_____
_____
_____
_____
_____
_____
_____
_____
_____
_____
_____

Do your good works now because
you might not make it back!

_____
_____
_____
_____
_____
_____
_____
_____
_____
_____
_____

If you want the Lord to have mercy on you when you fall on your knees,
you must first surrender your burdens unto him.… *Totally*

_____
_____
_____
_____
_____
_____
_____
_____
_____
_____
_____
_____
_____
_____
_____

Sooth your soul ... **SING** and
DANCE and *PEACE* will follow!
Put on your favorite artist and let your spirit flow.

When you don't understand,
seek a higher power and you'll never go wrong!
Sometimes regardless of our location,
we need to seek **HIM**.

When you know prayer, fear has no place.
Take the time.

What about *God's Grace*, is it
sufficient enough for you and your family?
What did grace do for you and yours?

_____

_____

_____

_____

_____

_____

_____

_____

_____

_____

_____

_____

_____

_____

_____

_____

_____

_____

_____

_____

_____

_____

_____

_____

_____

_____

_____

_____

_____

_____

_____
_____
_____
_____

_____
_____
_____
_____
_____
_____
_____

When life doesn't make sense—do the following:
Stick with it, Trust God, and **Pray**.
There's no better plan!

_____
_____
_____
_____
_____
_____
_____
_____
_____
_____
_____
_____
_____
_____
_____
_____
_____

If you had to teach a child to pray,
what would you say?

Until you learn to surrender, you're never going to get there.

Members want to have their way
while disciples let **GOD** have **HIS** way.
If you are a part of something,
be totally committed—don't just belong.

Which is more important in your life ~
Ethics or **Morals**?
Is there a difference?

_____

_____

_____

_____

_____

_____

_____

_____

_____

_____

_____

_____

_____

_____

_____

_____

_____

_____

_____

_____

_____

_____

_____

_____

_____

_____

There are many tragedies in **ALMOST**.
So stop "*almost*" doing things.
It's like saying you almost made a shot,
but the fact is you missed it.
Let's have some ownership.

If Christ would have **almost** given His life for us, where would we be? Don't be an almost person.

If **GOD** had been caught up in the tragedy of almost,
we'd be like a ship without a sail.

DRIFTING....

_____
_____
_____
_____
_____
_____
_____
_____
_____
_____
_____
_____
_____
_____
_____
_____
_____
_____
_____
_____
_____
_____
_____
_____
_____
_____

Will anyone **gain** a soul without selling theirs?
Too often, we lower our standards just to fit in.
Perhaps today you will choose to stand **FIRM**.

The greatest whispers
in the world are the
sunsets and sunrises.
They just wrap around your soul.
Take time to feel the beauty.

A well without water is like a heart without love.

EMPTY

What is the status of your heart?

Is it 30% love and 70% malice?

Did God take *his* rib so she could protect *her* heart?

When you leave the temple,
bring the tools with you!
Today I am working on:

Those in great churches must come from behind the walls and go to work. **To whom much is given, much is expected!** Right?

Is there something strange about the people at church having the same conversations as the people in the beauty salons and barbershops? *Should they be different?*

If the church is in your heart, what are those million dollar places people gather in on Sundays? Just filling stations. Right!

If **GOD** specializes, stop trying to assist Him.

Let go and let GOD.

IF you believe God uses people, then stop talking
about those who are doing good work,
regardless of where it is.
They're still looking after HIS sheep.

Silence is not always a failure to connect.
Sometimes, it is an emotional massage.

_____

_____

_____

_____

_____

_____

_____

_____

_____

_____

_____

In spirituality, love is worth the pain.
Think of what **JESUS** did!
What are you doing for **HIM**?

_____

_____

_____

_____

_____

_____

_____

_____

_____

_____

_____

_____

_____

_____

_____

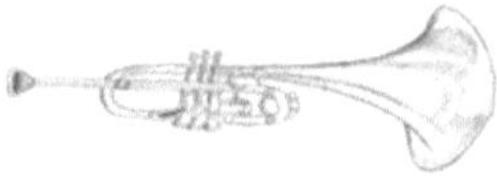

978-0-595-45554-6
0-595-45554-9

www.ingramcontent.com/pod-product-compliance
Lightning Source LLC
Chambersburg PA
CBHW030349290526
45785CB00004B/1664